18 kittens!

MOO! says
the COW.
Here's a stumper:
How long is a bus,
from bumper
to bumper?

How many toy **planes**, end to end, match the wings of *this* feathered friend?

7 toy planes!

How long is an otter? Do you know?

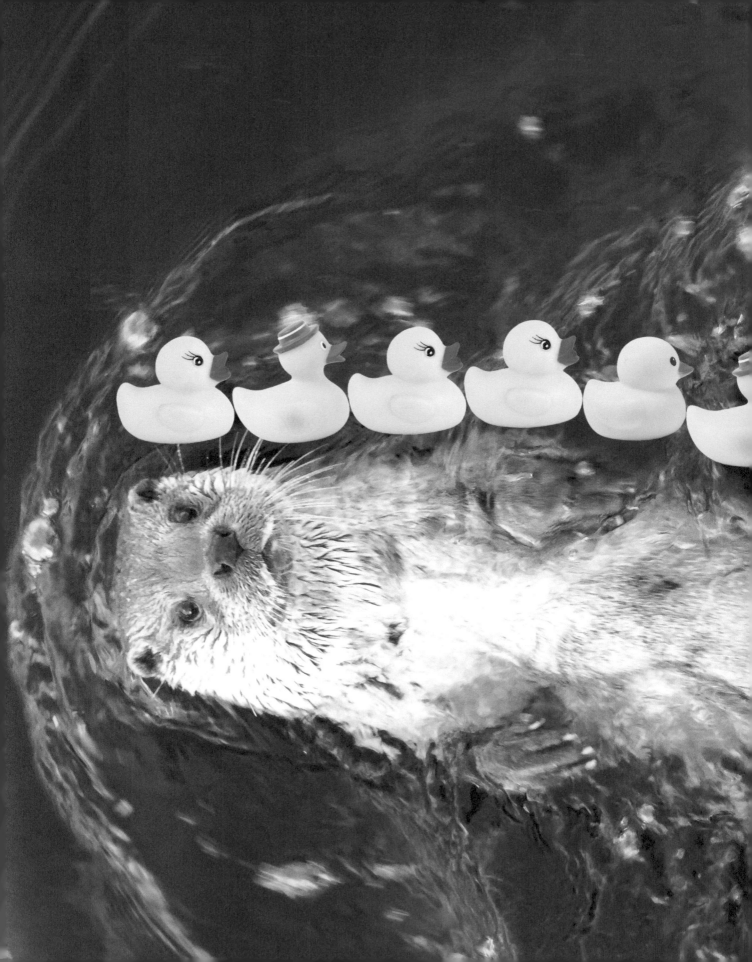

12 rubber
duckies,
head to toe!

Let's measure this **tail**, 1-2-3! How many gumballs would it be?

20 gumballs!

Here's an idea
that sounds
a bit weird:
Use a **bird**
to measure
a beard!

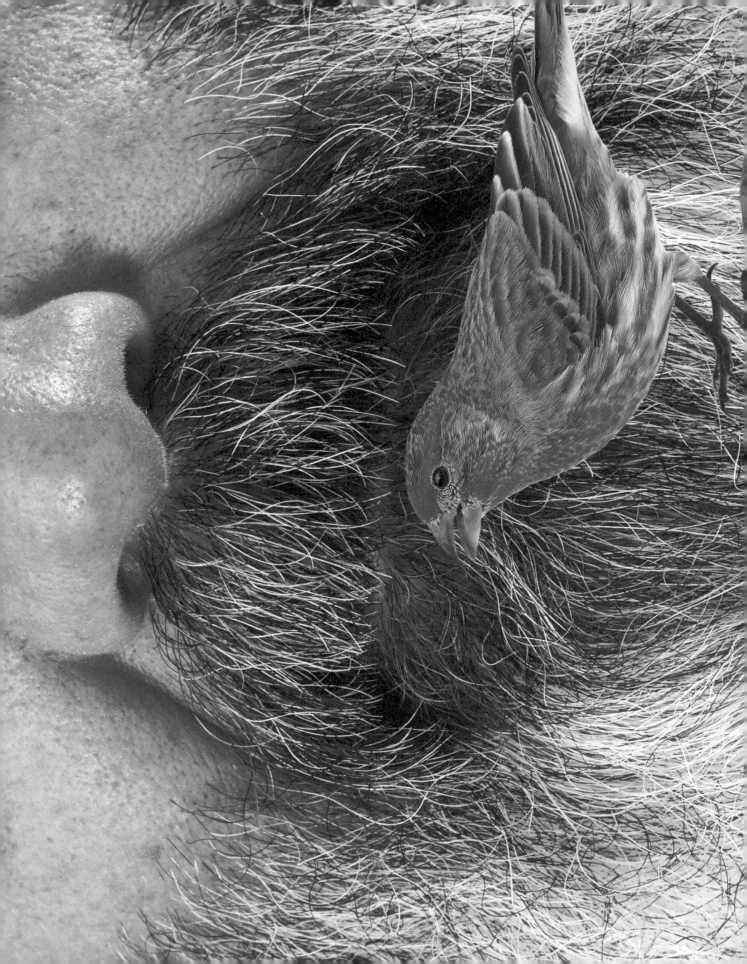

This beard is 3 birds long!

Measuring a **crayon** is a piece of cake! How many inchworms would it take?

4 inchworms!

Is this statement a lie or a truth? A **mouse** is as long as a lion's tooth.

TRUTH!

LOOK FOR OTHER BOOKS IN THE SERIES:

Pebble Sprout is published by Pebble, an imprint of Capstone.
1710 Roe Crest Drive, North Mankato, Minnesota 56003
www.capstonepub.com

Library of Congress Cataloging-in-Publication Data
Names; Cella, Clara, author.
Title; How many kittens could ride a shark? ; creative ways to look at length / by Clara Cella.
Description; North Mankato, Minnesota; Pebble, [2020] | Series; Silly measurements | Audience; Ages 4-6 | Audience; Grades K-1 | Summary;Introduce pre-readers to the math concept of length with eight goofy, non-standard measuring units, including kittens, toy airplanes, and gumballs. Delightful composite photos and a sprinkling of text illustrate the length of a shark, a lemur tail, a crayon, and more;— Provided by publisher.
Identifiers; LCCN 2019043573 (print) | LCCN 2019043574 (ebook)
   ISBN 9781977113238 (hardcover) | ISBN 9781977120106 (paperback) | ISBN 9781977113276 (ebook pdf)
Subjects; LCSH; Length measurement—Juvenile literature.
Classification; LCC QC102 .C45 2020 (print) | LCC QC102 (ebook) | DDC 530.8—dc23
LC record available at https;//lccn.loc.gov/2019043573 LC ebook record available at https;//lccn.loc.gov/2019043574

Image Credits
Shutterstock: 5 Second Studio, 4 (gray kitten), 5, almond, 20–21 (lemur), Anest, 28 (stretched inchworm), 29, Anna Utekhina, cover (cat's paws), 1, Charles Brutlag, 23, 24 (finch), 25 (finches), CLS Digital Arts, 29 (inchworm), ConstantinosZ, 12 (red, white, and blue toy plane), cynoclub, 4 (Bengal kitten), 5, Dmitry Kalinovsky, 4 (dark orange tabby kitten), 5, Dx09, 9 (front left), Eric Isselee, 3, 8 (front left and right), 9 (front right), 11, 30, 31 (mouse), Ewa Studio, 4 (orange tabby kitten), 5, GrashAlex, 12 (red toy plane), 13, GrigoryL, 4 (striped kitten), 5, Jay Bo, 31 (lion), Kitch Bain, 20 (gumballs), 21, Luis_Vazquez, 28–29 (crayons), Lukas Walter, 4–5 (shark), M Kunz, 7, Mtsaride, 27, Nerthuz, cover (top), back cover, Picsfive, 16 (rubber duck with eyelashes), 17, Randy van Domselaar, 15, ReaLiia, 12 (blue toy plane), 13, Sebastian Reinholdtsen, 16–17 (otter), sebra, 24–25 (bearded face), Sergey Uryadnikov, 12–13 (eagle), silky, 8–9 (bus), Sittirak Jadlit, 16 (plain rubber duck), 17, Tony Campbell, 4 (white and gray tabby kittens), 5, tratong, 19, Tsekhmister, 16 (rubber duck with blue hat), 17, Yuliia Sonsedska, cover (cat), 1

Editorial Credits
Editor: Jill Kalz; Designer: Ted Williams; Media Researcher: Svetlana Zhurkin; Production Specialist: Katy LaVigne

Printed in the United States   5743